WEEPING AND LAUGHING

POEMS OF GRIEF AND JOY

OLUSOLA SOPHIA ANYANWU

OCTOBER 2005

Copyright © Olusola Sophia Anyanwu 2025

The right of Olusola Sophia Anyanwu to be identified as author of this work has been asserted by her in accordance with the Copyright, Designs and Patents Act 1988.

All rights reserved.

No part of this publication may be reproduced or transmitted in any form or by any means, electronic or mechanical, including photocopy, recording, or any information storage and retrieval system, without permission in writing from the publisher.

www.olusolasophiaanyanwuauthor.com

*This work of art is dedicated to Pastor Victor Lambert
for his divine suggestion to write this book,
which helped me process my grief in 2005.*

Contents

Author's Notes	3
PART 1: WEEPING	5
1. Stroke	7
2. Ma Beatrice	9
3. Last Breath	13
4. Death Struck At 70	14
5. Birthday Eve!	16
6. Monster	18
7. Post Mortem	20
8. An Eyewitness	21
9. Was Yem Ready Or Not?	23
10. Is this a woman's life scenario?	28
11. Dirge to Mother's passing	30
12. She	32
13. Departure To Higher Glory	33
14. Like Jesus	34

PART 2: LAUGHING	35
15. My Memory of Mum	37
16. Letter To Mum	47
17. Mother	49
18. My Memory of Dad	51
19. Father	60
20. Letter to Dad	62
About The Poet	67
Other books by Olusola Sophia Anyanwu	69
Poetry	70

Author's Notes

These poems were written in 2005 when I was in grief and needed to heal over the loss of my beloved, precious, dear mother in October 2005. The poems in the Weeping section are written in times of weeping and anguish, but joy and laughter come in the end. The poems in the Laughter section prove our Lord Jesus Christ's victory over death and our hope for reunion with our beloved departed in eternity.

PART 1: WEEPING

1. Stroke

What is a stroke?
I don't know!
Many people do not quite know.
My mother did not quite know.
First, it killed her left leg.
Then, it killed her left arm.
She was helped to sit up.
Helped to the toilet and assisted.
Helped to the bathroom and bathed.
Helped to get dressed.
What a shameless sickness!
What a shameful sickness!
What a dehumanising sickness!
What a frustrating sickness!

What are you doctors doing?
What are you scientists doing?
Hurry up!!!
Find out what stroke is!
Find out how to get rid of it.
You might be next, and you won't quite know!

2. Ma Beatrice

Beatrice died on October 8th in Akure, Nigeria.
She was alive in the morning, afternoon and evening of that day.
None of her five children saw her except Avovo, her fourth.
Boberu, her first, was in London.
Her second, Stegomiah, was in London.
Her third, Loafy, was in Lagos.
Her fifth, Pugi, was visiting with Boberu in London.
Her fourth? Avovo or KK. Very painful.

KK arrived from London on 8th October
Straight from the Nigerian airport, in Lagos,
then straight to Ibadan
to East Wing 2 at University College Hospital.

Mum was surrounded by her
3 sisters, 3 nieces and 2 sister in-laws.
Mum was glad to see KK
but not excited.

Her other children were not present!
She asked after each one of them.
KK said, 'Bobe will come on the 16th,
Stegomiah on the 20th,
Pugi would come on the 25th
But Loafy would come tomorrow, the 9th.

Mum's temp was 240/80 - way above normal.
Her beautiful hairdo loosened for the head scan.
A jaw beard had grown.
She looked unkempt.
Her left hand was dead and cold.
Her eyes lost, distant, devoid of life -
not understanding her true situation.
KK phoned me then at 6 pm.
I did not understand what a stroke is.
We learnt that she was half-paralysed.
She could no longer bathe, feed, or sit.
She had bedsores on her back.
We hoped and prayed.
We prayed and hoped…

KK broke down and cried, 'Mummy! Mummy!
Her sisters had been looking after her.
They were her eyes, nose, mouth, ears and hands.
They always said to me or my sister, 'Your mother is fine.
It is just a lazy left leg.
KK wept with sorrow, discontent, despair and shock to see Mum's condition.
She questioned our aunts.
They said they had been feeding her with hope till her children arrived…

She got Mum bathed, changed, fed
and sorted out her medication.
Mum was now stable.
At 7.30 pm, she told Mum -
'I'm going to settle and unpack.
I promise to return immediately.'
Mum said, '' KK, stay with me,'
she urged her further.
KK did not understand.
'I will be back.'

KK checked into a hotel.
30 minutes later, she was called back.
Mum was gone!

Mum died with a prayer to God:
'Have mercy on my children.'
As a physician, KK certified Mum dead.
Bedlam broke loose.
Mum's sisters wailed and began to pray
for Mum to be returned to life.
At home in London
with my family and Pugi,
the phone rang at 8 pm.
It was KK.
'Boberu, Mum is dead…'
We received a numbing shock
padded without reality.

3. Last Breath

All of a sudden,
I was released from all pain.
I gasped for breath.
Then I knew in a second,
it was Death who had come.
I should have realised sooner.
I had only one second
to lift a prayer to my maker.
I felt no pain. I understood.
I was expiring my last breath.
I was heading for the Great Beyond.
I saw my Guardian Angel.
I bid the Earth my final bye.
I followed its direction to my eternal home.
To meet my Creator and Maker!

4. Death Struck At 70

Ma Beatrice died at 70.
She had known good and evil.
She had experienced triumph and defeat.
She had seen better and worse.
She had felt richness and poverty.

She had embraced independence and dependence.
She had touched humility and pride.
She had lived a life and survived all its consequences.
    At 70, she faced Death.
It crawled slowly towards her.
It gave her nightmares at night.
It fed her with pity at daylight.
It took her dignity away.
It stole her left arm and limb.

She was helpless, defenceless –
A pathetic figure trying to deny reality,
fighting a losing battle with courage and respect.

She died at 70.
She died without shedding a tear.
She died with prayers on her lips
for my siblings and me.
She died on the eve of my birthday.
She died on Saturday night.
She died on October 8, 2005.
She died at 70 years young.

Death did not use cancer,
Aids, Hepatitis, malaria, old age, sorrow,
heart failure, plane or car accident, childbirth, fire,
water, lightning, poison, witchcraft, pain or...

It faced her with a stroke
on the 16th of September and
killed her on the 8th of October.

5. Birthday Eve!

Early in the morning of October 8th, Sharon, my bosom friend in the US, phoned. 'HAPPY BIRTHDAY'. She said, 'I want to be the first to say it. That same evening, Folake, my sister, phoned. She said, 'Sister Sola, Mummy is dead!'

I was stunned in speechless silence for several seconds…

During that spell of time, my brain got damaged emotionally. I didn't say:

- Pray for her
- Shout the blood of Jesus Christ
- Put the phone to her ear, I want to call her
- Don't keep her in the morgue for 2 days
- Don't cry

- Sing to God
- Etc

No, I didn't do all these. I accepted the news, tried to ponder its meaning, weigh the consequences, and find answers to questions about why she had gone; why she had to go then, why she went without a sign, hint, clue, or message. Even a dream! Where she was, where she was going, how she faced death, when she first encountered death, the first premonitions before death took over… And all the suffering and indignity she had passed through before the fatal blow of Death.

6. Monster

Monster – what are you? What is your real name? What is your purpose for visiting people? True, you do not inflict bodily pain, fevers or headaches – BUT you steal life in slices. You treat a human being like food to be devoured. You eat a limb, then a hand, and then you swallow everything whole.
You are a monster!
You are evil!
What is good about you?
You took my precious mother away. She was destined to be a great grand mum.
You take precious children away.
You take our beloved family members away.
But there is One you can never take.
He defeated you.

He will take back all you took –
Our prosperity, health, wealth, loved ones and our souls.
When you take me, I will be restored.
To eternal life.
To Jesus.
FOREVER IN PEACE.

7. Post Mortem

I was not myself
– just a moving phantom,
full of confusion,
full of unsolved puzzles,
full of unresolved conflicts,
in total loss of all my senses,
in total loss of all coordination,
in total loss of all sense of responsibility.
It was by God's grace,
the feat of the burial ceremony,
was accomplished,
by God to His glory.

8. An Eyewitness

I had just got into Nigeria. Then I went straight to East Wing 2 at the University College Hospital in Ibadan to see Granny. She was surrounded by three sisters, three nieces, two sisters-in-law, and my aunt in a public ward. She was glad to see me, but I was horrified. I noticed that she was excited to see me, but she was very disappointed not to see any of her children present. I thought to console her with the dates her children would come, but she was not impressed.

My aunt said her temperature was above normal. Her beautiful hair had been removed for the head scan. A beard had grown. She looked unkempt. Her left hand was dead and cold, and her eyes lost, distant, devoid of life and understanding of her dire situation…

I broke down and cried, 'Granny! Granny!'

My Aunt bathed, dressed, and tidied her appearance, then transferred her to a private ward. There she fed Granny. It was 7.30 pm. Then I bade Granny a good night and promised to be with her the next morning.

Was Granny waiting for this? Thirty minutes later, Granny died with a prayer to God for His mercy on her children and grandchildren. My relatives and I could not accept the doctor's verdict of DEATH. We all began to talk to God in different languages, in the hope that God would resurrect Granny. But Granny never came back to life…

9. Was Yem Ready Or Not?

Yem [Oghoyemwe] was to be mourned on the 16th and buried on 17th of November.
She was fourth out of eight children.
She was a Benin woman who had followed God's destiny for her and found herself in Yoruba Land.
She was quiet, secretive, deep, friendly, emotional and 'unfriendly'.
She was a passionate woman, but if her volcano were upset, it would erupt hot coals of lava and brimstone.
Yes. When upset or rubbed on a raw side, Yem became bad-tempered, hot-tempered, and quick-tempered with words, becoming arrow-shaped and daggering at you.

Yem was a woman with some dreams unfulfilled in life, and even at death, the dreams evaded her.

You left your palace at Akure, 5, Ilaje Street, Ijapo Estate, where all your treasures lay under lock and key twenty-four hours a day.
When a stroke struck your limbs, you went to the hospital.
There, your queenly crown, jewels, robe and dignity were all stripped from you. Your kids were not around to hide your nakedness, shame, hurt, pain and sorrow.
Oh, Yem, you were surrounded by people who, like hawks and vultures, were waiting for the booty; visitors who stared in curiosity at a queen unveiled. You read their secret laughs at your blushing.

Yem, you gave up the spirit of your ghost, and your body was quickly put in a morgue. Your spirit returned seconds later to your body, horrified. It sped away in sorrow.
Strangers attended to your body! Where were your children when they bathe your nakedness and clothed you, your pants and bra? You were dressed.

Your body was transported to a morgue in Lagos, not with your kids, but with strangers, to be kept frozen where there was electricity.

Then back again to your palace without your orderly or a police escort.
There at your palace, you were awaited by your children, grandchildren, your siblings, your in-laws, your friends and well-wishers, for your burial.
Some others came to gain life from your death like parasites.
Some others came to observe 'all protocol', but I wept because of your dreams that evaded you in life and in death. Oh Yem!
And your kids? Some may have tried their best, but they were all lousy!
They did not clothe your nakedness; strangers did.
They did not visit you in the morgue; strangers did.
They did not travel with your body from Lagos to Akure; strangers did.
They deserted your palace, except your second daughter, for hotels after the wake-keeping.

There was no light.
No efficient organisation ensured there was light for 24 hours.

Some of your kids were very greedy, busy diverting burial funds into their own pockets.
Oh, Yem, how did you feel to see all this from wherever you were?
I hope you are completely above all human pain, all human desires, hatred, anger, and revenge.
Your sons – your coveted, precious males! What did they do?
Did they make you proud, or did they behave like strangers?
Did they behave like real people burying a beloved parent?
Were they worse off than visitors and strangers?
What did you think of your in-laws from the North, South, East and West? How do you judge your daughters?
Are you embittered by their ignorance, inadequacies, inefficiency, shortcomings, human weaknesses, pride or foolishness?
Oh Yem!

Then you were to be buried!
There was confusion about reception venues!
The whole ceremony, which started from A, then continued at B, and then finished at C! How clumsy!!

But Yem, let us thank God for everything.
You are with God now. How is your room in Heaven?
What is it like to have a heavenly body?
Are you allowed to see us?
Can you visit us in our dreams?
Where is your soul and spirit?
Can you see Dad, your own parents and other loved ones gone before you? What is it like to view the failings of humans on Earth?
– The 'amazing' and unnecessary flow of thoughts pumping out of our heads at alarming speed and frequency!
Are all these mysteries untied knots?
What are your pleasures now?
Yes, you are at rest.
Yes, you are free from Earth's evil.
Yes, you are free from Earth's pain.
Yes, you are free from Earth's strife.
But one thing I know.
Yem, you were not actually prepared to meet with Death on October 8, 2005.

10. Is this a woman's life scenario?

A woman is born.
She gets educated.
She gets married.
She gets children.
She lives for her husband.
She lives for her children.
Her husband gets other women.
Her husband gets other kids.
Her husband deserts her bed.
Then on the eve of her death,
Her husband offers her his true heart.

Her children leave the nest.
Her children go far, far, far away.
They get busy with life -

Getting educated,
Getting married,
Getting children,
Living for their children,
Living for their husbands,
Living for their wives,
Living for their children,
The woman gets sick.
Her children are not there.

The woman is dying.
Her children are not there.
The woman dies with no child at her bedside.
The woman is bathe by strangers.
The body is dressed by strangers.
At her burial, there is no unity amongst her children
The children she had strived so hard to protect and serve.
She worshipped them
She pampered them
BUT she forgot to draw any one of them close to her heart!

II. Dirge to Mother's passing

Your thoughts haunt me still.
Mother, do I know you?
So deep like a bottomless abyss
We could never reach you, know you, understand you…
What of that impregnable rock shield you cast around you
- To hide you, your identity and your heart?
How could I have known when Death called you?
You who always treated me like a princess –
A child never to be hurt, a child never to be made uncomfortable - when I was already a woman.
You hid your pain well. You knew you were crossing over.

You knew Arthritis did not strike your leg. You knew it was a stroke.

Even in your dream where Death warned you, you hid from me.

How fair is that to me?

In your eyes, you were fair.

Your princess must not see how the stroke struck off your left arm and foot.

Nor see the sores on your back, your sick bed was feeding from.

You shielded my eyes from such horror.

Such inhuman dignity, such misery, such a nightmare,

Such unquestionable frustration for a proud, healthy, beautiful woman, very educated –a Judge!

In your eyes, you were fair to keep the glorious image I had of my mother.

That is your gift. I still have it.

But my imaginative mind pictured you thousands of miles away

– What you must have gone through, endured, suffered…

You denied me the opportunity of being your nurse, of being your pastor, being your soldier and playing my role by you, as your first daughter.

Mother, this still haunts me.

12. She

She came as a daughter, sister, mother, mum, grandmother, stepmother and friend.
We thought She would live like Methuselah.
We thought She was as wise as Solomon.
We thought She was as strong as Samson.
We thought She was like the Holy Ghost to be with us always.
Then She went away suddenly and unexpectedly.
She left us all shocked, dumbfounded, flabbergasted, surprised, astonished, puzzled, confused and miserable!
But for God's sake, we will not ask 'WHY?'
We will praise God and learn the precious lessons He wants us to understand.
She was precious. Thanks, Mum.

13. Departure To Higher Glory

Mum went yesterday to Heaven
We will meet her tomorrow in Heaven
We will not ask why she went yesterday and not later
We know now that Death is real
It is ugly
It is not accountable to any man
It makes us learn lessons
from mistakes and life
So, thanks Mum for yesterday and yesteryears
The memories are rich and cherished

14. Like Jesus

Mummy, like Jesus, has gone
To make us free
To make us safe
To bring blessings
To make life easier

PART 2: LAUGHING

Celebration of Mum's Memory
[January 1936 - October 2005]

15. My Memory of Mum

I see Mum in my dream
as if she were still part of our world!
Thank God for yesterday and thank God for TODAY.
I am alive to celebrate Mum's memory!
Mum seemed to be everlasting.
Mum, I was just getting to understand you, like we were sisters.
You were a woman who was just beginning to discover
another woman in her daughter.
A woman in your eyes who still seemed like a child
to be sheltered, pampered, shielded from the perplexities of life
including the mysteries of you!

However today,
I am not like the walking zombie going through
your funeral ceremony.
Time has given me this opportunity by God's grace
to relieve the memory of her who bore me
in a virginal birth at the age of twenty-two.
I remember her as my father's wife.
She was ever busy and dutiful,
being the great house manager –
supervising maids, cooks, washermen, drivers,
gardeners, and security personnel. The big houses
with lively kids – yet always clean.
I remember her getting everywhere
to dust, polish, clean and tidy out rooms.

I remember the days she went to the market
forever and endlessly inspecting every item.
I remember her washing vegetables and meat
meticulously.
I remember food and meals served hot and palatable.
Her children's clothes are well laundered.
They were always well-dressed for church and
parties.
She was a homely mother – knitting, sewing and
baking cakes

to welcome her children from swimming and various outings.
She had her perfect moods.
She told stories and taught us songs like:
Day by Day, Dear Lord of the three things I pray: to see thee more clearly, love thee more dearly, follow thee more nearly, day by day. Amen.

The best stories - her childhood days with her parents,
her school days at St Annes,
the love she had for her Dad and her senior stepbrothers, Sam and David.
She kept poultry and grew vegetables.
She reared rabbits, monkeys, dogs and cats.
She tended these with devotion and energy.
My father enjoyed life like a king in a palace:
Special dishes with hot food at the high table.
She served my father.
Her family ate daily at a table properly set with cutlery and serviettes,
She expected and observed the correct dining etiquette.

I saw a true Capricornia putting hot water
into the dishes to heat them before the food is put in.

I saw a very resourceful wife never throwing anything away-
empty cans, bottles, jars, packets, newspapers, eggshells…
I saw a wonderful wife despite upheavals from work as a lawyer,
kept the home clean, conducive, charming and inviting.
I saw a security-conscious wife ensuring maximum safety:
Locking up the stores, bedrooms, cupboards...
I saw her going to the far corners of Gbagi, Oritamerin, Oja Oba, Aperin
- to get the best sales and deals for the house, family and food.

I remember a passionate, loving mother
whose words were coated with endearments –
'darling, sweetheart, to her children and oko mi[for her husband],
Ede nomono[pet name for my youngest sister],
Woye mi[pet name for my younger brother],
Sholly [pet name for me],
Folly or KK[pet name for my younger sister],
Ori mi[my head] pet name for my younger brother],
used rarely and on very special occasions of success.

She had a special bedroom name for my dad, but in front of the family, she called him –'Daddy'.

We were all very dear to her
each of us groomed to be a special individual
with their own unique personality.
I remember my own bed, my own cupboard
my own table seat, my own car seat, my own dog and hen!
I remember her laughter.
She was humorous, witty and could enjoy a good joke.
I remember her watching 'Petticoat Junction' and 'I Dream of Jeannie' in the 1960s
She preferred watching TV movies to swimming or going out to parties.

I remember with nostalgia her Saturday visits to me, as a boarder at Yejide Girls Grammar School, Ibadan.
I remember her communicating with her eyes with us children
I remember the occasional 'Pele Sholly'
after being assigned a domestic task.
I remember June 1973, a special visit in school.

She brought me Eggovin, several pieces of fried
chicken, and a double portion of all the goodies to
mark my entry into womanhood!
I remember my mum -
a stern, severe, too strict disciplinarian, with me.

She was particular about personal hygiene,
Perfect habits in eating, drinking, walking,
dressing, speaking, sitting and standing,
toileting and bathing, playing and sleeping,
gentlemen's habits, such as males not crying, and
male ego and dominance…
She did get very cross when any of these habits was
breached.
This was often the case for me because I was a
tomboy of sorts.
I remember her being impeccably well-dressed,
both at work and at home.
She could not stand shoddy and cheap appearances.

I remember her love for animals.
Stray dogs accepted into our household uninvited.
She tolerated Dad's fancy for monkeys and
a daughter's love for rabbits.
She had love for the chickens and cats.
Her first son dared to buy a crocodile!

But this croc was turned out
on 9th November 1969.
I remember all the photographs she took with our pets.

I remember Mum when she was happy.
She would sing [in her melodious voice],
had loving words for everyone,
gave leave from challenging tasks and
prepared very special meals.
I heard her native Edo language on the phone with her siblings.

I remember that for most of my life
Mum tried to understand me
and make me understand her.
I remember her keeping very guardedly
my first term exam answer sheets from secondary school.
I noticed she kept all the letters I ever wrote to her
from the days of my life as a boarding student.

I remember my trip to the UK and Italy in 1977
with Mum.
I realised how much she appreciated success.
She treated me always like a royal queen.

I remember she asked me to ride her back
when I passed successfully into the University of Ife.
At the time, she was frying meat outside
in the backyard of our home.
She grabbed a big piece and put it in my hand to eat.
I remember her buying two big suitcases of clothes
to start university life!
I remember my first sewn lace, gifted to me by Mum
to mark my 21st birthday.

I remember her love and honour for God.
She always kept new money notes
to give as offerings in church
I remember she laid out the trinkets
my sisters and I would wear to church and social
engagements.
I remember her generosity to the clergy:
She never visited them empty-handed.
They never left her home empty-handed.
She believed in giving to her in-laws, her family and
extended family.
I remember her standing and looking regal beside
my father in church
as she sang in her high, solo voice.
Her Estee lauder perfume filled my nostrils.
She was a praying woman:

I saw and heard her pray in the Edo language
in the morning and at the end of the day.
She prayed when we faced exams and life challenges.

I remember my mum crying
When her in-laws came to collect me
after my traditional wedding ceremony at 9 pm.
I remember being shocked to find Mum
hiding near the kitchen area and cleaning tears off
her face.
Then I realised how much I meant to my mum
despite the harsh discipline I had constantly
received growing up.
I remember my mum had fainted from anxiety
waiting for her children to arrive at her home from
the UK
in November 2004 for my dad's funeral.
I will never forget the way she had looked…

I remember my mum as a grandmother to my kids:
very attentive to them and buying them smart
clothes.
She bought lots of toys. They ate what they loved.
She pampered them.
They called her 'Granny'.

I remember that she held my husband and in-laws in esteem.

I remember her burial. It had been a sober farewell. Her people from Benin and in-laws came to bid her farewell.

She had just turned 70 that year and was in good health until stroke struck.

Her exit was a rude shock to all her loved ones.

She finally departed Earth and returned to God in Heaven

on the 8th of October 2005, and

buried on the 18th of November,2005.

Her husband, our Dad,

Died October 17 and buried November 26th, 2004!

The coincidence of it all with October and November!

16. Letter To Mum

Dear Mum,
I have been comforted by the peace of God that passeth all understanding. I'm healed by God's grace, which has been sufficient for me. I no longer mourn in ignorance. I acknowledge who you are with - JESUS! I'm comforted that we'll meet in eternity with our Papa God.

I have written a poem each for you and Dad to honour you both in 'Chameleon and Other Poems'. I have written a novel that tells the beautiful and touching story of your life and Dad's entire life story. [Their Journey on Earth to Heaven]

The photographs of both you and Dad are placed for all to see on the walls of my home. I still have albums of you both and our family, which I browse through from time to time. Continue to enjoy the perfect peace of living eternally in Heaven.

Guess what, Mum! Well, you are a divine being.
You already know.
I just want you to smile. From your five children, you have fourteen grandchildren.
From your grands, you have forty great grands and still counting!
All is well, Mum!

You will ever be remembered!
You will never be forgotten!

Love from your,
Asholly Pepper.

My poem for you, Mum

17. Mother

Mother of five
Wife to our father
Our source of existence
That channelled five seedlings
Through a pure gate
Our greatest gift
Your five gifts are to you
Your existence and treasure

May you find in them
All that would please you
All that will gladden you
May you find in their existence

A pride to you
May you find your existence
Worthy of living through them

May they be to you
Your stored up treasures that will
Multiply your pride and blood
May the mouths you fed never bite you

Celebration of Dad's memory
[December 1925 - October 2004]

18. My Memory of Dad

I thank God for today:
In Heaven, Dad and Mum are at peace and in love.
I'm alive to celebrate their memory.
He was named Augustus, Oladipo Ebenezer Adebayo.
Born on 31st December in Igbaroke in Western Nigeria.
Nick named Bonny by his wife,
Named Adidi Cougar by his children and
Artful Dodger to his close friends.

Today is a celebration of the memory of loved ones.
Dear, precious Dad departed to higher glory on October 17, 2004.
My Dad was buried like a King and a hero.

The whole town was involved.
Gunshots had heralded the dawn of his burial…
Today, I remember Dad:
Dad played the piano every day.
I still hear the tunes in my soul – of Bohemian
Melody, Classical Melody, Sabbath Melody and
Cujus Animam
He gave us piano lessons from Smallwood's Piano
Tutor
Always in his study room before 7 am,
doing his devotion, writing or reading.

I remember him immaculately dressed up in a suit
to go to work.
A Big man in government, but never too tired for us.
He returned to give his children lessons and during
weekends,
swimming, zoos, strolling, partying, hoteling,
or shopping for storybooks or new clothing in the
stores.
I remember the story told about his life,
his teaching us Psalms 23, 121, 27, 90
and the Yoruba song - 'Tewo bebe wa'.
I remember the corporal discipline for us children
for forgetting to:

do homework, greet, keep things tidy, obey
and for not coming in the first three positions.

He was a very considerate man.
He was never seen in an open quarrel with Mum.
He was a lover of harmony, peace, nature,
animals, beauty and gardening.
A very Englishman to the letter:
polite to house helps, colleagues and all junior staff.
He didn't play the boss or head of the family to his advantage.
A true hero. Impartial. He was a rewarder of the faithful.
Generous to those who opened their hearts in love to him.
I remember my vacation to Italy in 1977 with my mother,
for passing my convocation entrance exams to Unife.
I remember his love for comedy: Baba Sala programmes.
I remember him watching the Carry-On series with Mum.

My DAD – in March 1983, came all the way from Ibadan to Makurdi

8 hours away, when I was in trouble. [Baby coming before wedlock!]
In December 1974, he came to Yejide, my secondary school,
picked me out from amongst my schoolmates,
for my trip to the church for my confirmation in his Mercedes.
My classmates had looked on in surprise, some in envy.
He gave me good reason to keep his memory alive in my heart.
In August 1987, he sponsored Chima, my husband and me
to the UK for two weeks.
He made the long 8-plus-hour journeys from the West to the East
after each of my childbirths. Once to check up on me!
He always made me so proud with the fat cash gifts.
An excellent family man, he was.
I remember how Christmas, New Year, Easter and Birthdays were spent.
– Lots of feasting, music and heart-warming presents!

I remember the entire family trip to the UK in 1975.
I remember him visiting me in the hospital with books:
'Tiptoes the mischievous kitten' and 'Micky the disobedient puppy' in 1967.
I started to love the idea of books then.
I remember Dad giving us children cold shower baths
to cool off our hot body temperature.
I remember visits to Dr Khan for a malaria jab, in his car.
I remember the golden handshakes for memorising a psalm or at piano lessons.
I remember the embraces and hugs and his pride from our great deeds of academic accomplishments.
I remember his joy from our academic success and advancements.
I learnt the Yoruba proverb, 'Aigbofa ni a wo oke; ifa kan ko si ni para' -
'One who does not know something and looks at the ceiling, but the answers are not written there!'
which he always said
when I struggled in my maths and English lessons with him.
I remember the bicycles and big toy cars he got us when we were kids.

I remember a dad,
Despite being very busy with government work life,
carved out a lot of time to cherish, love, care and pamper us
in such a way that his memory will always be a celebration.
I remember the weekend trips to play in the lagoon in Lagos
I remember Green Springs Hotel and Cocodome for swimming
One of the most beautiful and precious memories which will extend even to my generations and unborn generations in future
is my receiving letters, birthday cards, and gifts up until September 2004.
He died the following month that same year!!
A man well over 75 devoted time and energy
to writing to me constantly and remembering my birthday!!
He always addressed me as 'Sholly Baby'!
I remember my 21st birthday present of N500 from Dad in 1979!
I remember the car he got me after my NYSC,
For my first teaching job in Port Harcourt in 1982.
I remember how I went to Port Harcourt for the first time to start my teaching career, with two cars.

One carried my luggage,
the other vehicle carried me, Teddy and Kinky, my two dogs.
If I can but even achieve one tenth of the virtues of this great man,
I would consider myself as famous as a celebrity!
A first-class brain from the University of Ibadan in 1955,
An elder top statesman of government,
A lecturer of political science and an associate dean
A District Officer of the old Western Nigeria,
A father of eight children,
A grandfather to twenty-one grandchildren
A pillar in All Souls' Church, Bodija - ahh, how grateful I would be!
I remember Dad's love for reading and his grand library of books
with knowledge from all works of life.
I remember Dad's talent for writing.
He authored and published eight books [I have read them all now, but not then]–
all displayed proudly in my home library and other parts of the world.

I remember:
Stories and tales of his life blessed my growing years.

His devotion to God, our Father Almighty,
his love for Songs of Praise, Hymnal Companion
and leading church groups.
I remember my adoration and admiration
of him dressed gloriously on Sundays beside my mother,
on their favourite specific pew in church.
I remember his love for classical music, particularly
his playing of Jerusalem, Windsor Forest, Bach,
Beethoven, and Handel on the stereo record player.
These sent me on such lofty daydreams where I saw
myself in my glory…
I remember his teaching us lessons in English and
maths, and hearing
We read stories from 'Stories from Ancient Civilisations'.
I remember with pride the family photograph taken
on my 13th birthday.
I remember him playing draughts with my husband.
I remember him listening to fantasy stories from
my children's lips,
His keen interest in my writings, as he read all my
manuscripts.
Today, I thank God for giving me the gift of writing,
just like My Dad.

I remember his love of photography - captured memories of
our childhood, adulthood, family life and his every decade.
He gave me a photo portrait of himself, which is still hanging on the wall.
My only regret is that he hid his pains from me…

I did not realise he was already an old man,
already on his journey to the celestial realms,
when I last saw him alive, in April 2004…

Dad,
continue to rest in peace
in your higher and greater glory.
Your memory
will ALWAYS remain loved,
cherished and evergreen
till we meet
in eternity
forever and ever
and ever…

My poem for you, Dad!

19. Father

FARMER,
You have deposited your seeds,
May you reap what you sow.

You have been embraced with
Intellect, wisdom and art
May they give you peace of heart.
To your legal seedlings
You have done your duty.
May they honour you in return

Farmer,
With many farms and seeds
May you never be confused and alienated.
Regret shall not be your lot.
May life continue to shower,
Her mercies and blessings on you.

Finally, lead you in peace at the end.

20. Letter to Dad

Hi Daddy,

Thanks for visiting me in my dreams. You always look so lovely. I see Mum too, but I didn't tell her! You know how superstitious she is. I don't want her thinking that I think she is a witch! Dad, I hear you laugh. Bless you for your humour and laughter. Your bulgy eyes twinkling with unspoken mirth! How is our Papa God? I know it's a secret to say what He looks like.

Nobody on Earth has been to Heaven and back here to tell Heavenly tales, about life there in Heaven, Dad!

I know you must have broken the rules and told me God's secret. There are no more penalties as eternity is final. Keep trying, Dad. I trust you must have told me Heaven's secrets, but oh dear! Our night escapades, rendezvous and adventures are deleted when I wake up. Do you know Nigeria is in a mess right now? I will not bore you with gory tales and gists. Please tell God to deliver Nigeria and other countries in conflict.

I want you to know how proud I am of you for the legacy you left behind for us, especially for me. Your footsteps are so big that I can't step in but guess what! I have also authored and published books. One of my sons made a first class like you, too. I have children who are as intelligent as you, too, in fields such as management, banking, medicine, and engineering.

My children teach their children to swim, to love books, to write stories, and to appreciate art and photography. Your great-grandson points to your picture on the wall. None of them has your bulgy eyes, which I love so much about you. They all have large expressive eyes. None of them will be short like you or me, Dad, but they will definitely leave their marks on the page of this Earth like you did! And I'm trying to do the same.

I teach my grands to play the piano, love dolls, toys, board games, books, and enjoy rides on the Queen Elizabeth train from Abbey Wood Station to Victoria and back! You can peep at us if God will allow you. My only regret is the painful fact that you and Mum did not encourage me to learn either Yoruba or Edo fluently. Now my children and grandchildren are following suit! Let's hope this changes.

How does it feel to reunite with your parents and siblings? Wow! Well, one day, when God decides, I shall reunite with you and Mum. Till then, have fun and take care.
All the best from your,
Sholly Baaaabe!

About the Poet

Olusola Sophia Anyanwu is an educationist, reviewer, encourager, bestselling author and poet. She loves reading books that grab her attention and interest. She says, "I love reading and writing stories that reflect the fascinating lives and relationships between people. Her writings also convey current issues in the world. She also writes Christian fiction and poetry to inspire hope and encouragement. The Holy Spirit of God inspires her. She is a member of the Association of Christian Writers [ACW], Society of Authors, National Poetry Library, Society of Poets, and TRELLIS Poetry Group, UK.

She has over 20 books published. As a multi-genre author and poet, she writes on various assorted themes about life. Her works have been featured in the ACW eNews,

ACW magazine, ACW blog, and the ACW Bookshop in the UK and Amazon. Olusola Sophia says, "I want my readers to be carried to lofty heights in the realms of passion, love, faith, adventure, and laughter as they read each of my books. So get a dig in!"

She hopes her writing creates a positive influence on readers, enriches their lives, and gives encouragement and blessings. She is married and blessed with children and grandchildren. She is on Twitter, Facebook, LinkedIn, TikTok, YouTube, Goodreads, Amazon, and Instagram. More about Sophia and her books can be found on her website:

www.olusolasophiaanyanwuauthor.com

Other books by Olusola Sophia Anyanwu

- Stories for Younger Generations
- Tales for Younger Generations
- Sophia's Fables for Younger Generations
- Stories for Older Generations
- Stories from the Heart
- The New Creatures
- We Can't Breathe
- Turning the Clock hands backwards
- The Confession
- The Crown
- Their Journey on Earth to Heaven
- The Robe
- The Captive's Crown
- Parables of Assorted Flavours

Poetry

- Chameleon and Other Poems
- Sophia's Covid Poetry
- Poetry from the Heart
- Elegies and Dirges
- Echoes of Eco
- From the Womb
- Wings of Faith
- Poetry Matters
- Sweet Slices of Life

www.ingramcontent.com/pod-product-compliance
Lightning Source LLC
Chambersburg PA
CBHW051714040426
42446CB00008B/872